Lewis Harcourt

An Eton Bibliography

Lewis Harcourt

An Eton Bibliography

ISBN/EAN: 9783337717391

Printed in Europe, USA, Canada, Australia, Japan

Cover: Foto ©ninafisch / pixelio.de

More available books at **www.hansebooks.com**

AN

ETON [...]

[...]

LONDON

[...]

1898

PREFACE.

The following pages are a first and, I fear, incomplete attempt at an Eton Bibliography.

They are mainly compiled from the catalogue of my own collection of " Etoniana " (destined ultimately for the School Library), to which I have added the titles of those books with whose names I am acquainted, but of which I do not yet possess copies: these entries I have distinguished with a dagger (†) in the hope that I may hear of copies of them for sale.

I have endeavoured as far as possible—and with considerable success—to discover and record the names of the authors of anonymous books and pamphlets and of the editors of the ephemeral School Magazines, but I have felt bound in printing this Bibliography to respect their anonymity.

There are, however, many anonymous authors still to be identified, and I shall gratefully receive any information on this subject, and by way of *addenda* to or *corrigenda* of the Bibliography.

I have intentionally omitted all School Text-books from the collection.

L. V. HARCOURT.

MALWOOD, LYNDHURST.

AN ETON BIBLIOGRAPHY.

1560. Three Sermons preached at Eaton Colledge. By Roger Hutcbinson. 1552. Pp. 110. Sm. 16mo. John Day, Aldersgate, London. 1560.

1572. Memoirs of the Eminent Persons educated in Eton College. By Thomas Hatcher. 2 vols. 1572. †

1626. *Testis Veritatis,* the Doctrine of King James, our late Soueraigne of famous memory : of the Church of England : of the Catholicke Church : plainly shewed to bee one in the points of predestination, free-will, certaintie of saluation. With a discouerie of the grounds both naturall and politicke of Arminianisme. By F. Rouse [Provost of Eton, 1644-59]. Pp. 107. Sq. cr. 8vo. Printed at London by W. I. 1626.

1651. *Reliquiae Wottonianae :* or a Collection of Lives, Letters, Poems ; with Characters of Sundry Personages : and other Incomparable Pieces of Language and Art. Also Additional Letters to Several Persons not before printed. By the curious pencil of the ever-memorable Sir Henry Wotton, Kt., Late Provost of Eton College. 1651. †

Second Edition. 1654. Third Edition, pp. 584. 12mo. T. Roycroft, London, 1672. Fourth Edition, with Additions of Several Letters to the Lord Zouch, never publish'd till now. Pp. 713. Sm. 8vo. B. Tooke, at the Ship in St. Paul's Churchyard, London. 1685. Wotton's letters to Lord Zouch occupy pp. 583-713.

1657.   A Christian Calendar for Children or Youth, or an Essay of laying down and in the Principles of Sound Doctrines, by way of Catechism in fifty-two weeks, calculated for the Scholars of Eton College (with their neighbours) by the present Catechist there.   London.   1657. †

1659.   Golden Remains of the Ever Memorable Mr. John Hales of Eton College, etc.   Pp. 326.   Sq. cr. 8vo.   T. Garthwait, London.   1659.

1680.   A Sermon preached at the Anniversary Meeting of the Eton Scholars at St. Mary-le-Bow, on 18th Nov., 1679.   By Thos. Horn.   4to.   Samuel. 1680. †

1684.   Forty Sermons, whereof twenty-one are now first published, the greatest part preached before the King and on solemn occasions.   By Richard Allestree, D.D., King's Professor in the Chair of Divinity in the University of Oxford, Provost of Eton and Chaplain to His Majesty.   Vols. I., II.   Pp. 254, 307.   Sm. roy. 4to.   R. Bentley, London.   1684.

[c. 1688.] A Sermon at Eton.   By Rev. S. Upman [Fellow of Eton]. †

1689.   Poems and Translations written upon Several Occasions, and to Several Persons.   By "A late Scholar of Eaton" [Charles Goodall].   Pp. 182. 12mo.   Henry Bonwicke, London.   1689.

1701.   A Sermon preached at St. Paul's Cathedral, before the Gentlemen educated at Eton and King's College, on 6th December, 1700.   By Knightley Chetwood, D.D., Archdeacon of York and late Fellow of King's College. Pp. 42.   Sq. post 8vo.   B. Tooke, London.   1701.

A Sermon preached before the Gentlemen educated at Eton College, at St. Austin's Church, London, on 6th December, 1701.   By William Fleetwood, Fellow of Eton College, and Chaplain in Ordinary to His Majesty. Pp. 22.   Sq. cr. 8vo.   Charles Harper, London.   1701. †

1702.   A Sermon preached at St. Paul's Cathedral, the 8th of Dec., 1702, before the Gentlemen educated at Eton College.   By J. Adams, Rector of St.

Alban, Wood Street, and Chaplain in Ordinary to Her Majesty. Pp. 23. Sm. 8vo. Thos. Bennett, London. 1702.

1704. Wisdom the Best Possession : a Sermon at Christ-Church at the Anniversary Meeting of the Gentlemen educated at Eton and King's College. By J. Rawson. 4to. 1704. †

1716. Several Tracts by the ever-memorable Mr. John Hales of Eaton College, etc., to which is added his Letter to Abp. Laud. Pp. 228. 16mo. 1716.

1717. A Letter to the Scholars of Eton ; occasioned by their Master, Dr. Snape's, Letter to the Bishop of Bangor. D.H. 12mo. Pp. 40. J. Roberts, London. 1717. †

A Rod for the Eton Schoolmaster's Back ; or a Letter from a Country Schoolboy to Dr. Snape, occasioned by one from him to the Bishop of Bangor. By which it seems that the said doctor was not at all qualified for what he undertook. Third ed. Pp. 24. 12mo. Roberts, Lond. 1717.†

Proposals for Printing by Subscription *Antiquitates et Athenæ Etonienses* in 4 vols. 8vo. By an Impartial Hand [Richard Rawlinson, D.D]. Specimen page. Fo. 1717. †

1719. An Historical and Critical Account of the Life and Writings of the ever-memorable Mr. John Hales, Fellow of Eton College and Canon of Windsor. Being a Specimen of an Historical and Critical English Dictionary. Pp. 96. R. Robinson, London. 1719.

1730. *Catalogus Alumnorum E Coll. Eton, in Coll. Regale Cantab. Cooptatorum.* 4to. Eton. 1730. †

1732. *Musae Juveniles.* By William Cooke, Head Master of Eton. Pp. 104. 8vo. Pote, Eton. 1732. †

1740. Charity, the great End and Design of Christianity : in a sermon preached at Eton by Zachary Cradock, D.D., late Provost of Eton College. Second edition. Pp. 31. Cr. 8vo. Olive Payne, London. 1740.

1745. Bill of Eton College and School [edited by E. C. Hawtrey]. 1745. †

1746. Sermon in the Collegiate Church at Eton, on the Suppression of the Rebellion. By T. Ashton. 4to. 1746. †

1747. Ode on Eton. By Thomas Gray. 4to. 1797. † Frequently reprinted.]

1750. *Elogium Famae Inserviens Jacci Etonensis, sive Gigantis;* or the Praises of Jack of Eton, commonly called Jack the Giant : Collected into Latin and English metre, after the manner of Thomas Sternhold, John Hop-kins, John Burton, and others. To which is added a Dissertation on the Burtonic Style. By a Master of Arts. Pp. 208. Sm. post 8vo. S. Parker, Oxford. 1750.

1755. *Musae Etonenses : sive Poematia in duos tomos distributa.* Vols. I., II. By J. Prinsep. I., pp. 152; II., pp. 120. Demy 8vo. J. Pote, *Etonae.* 1755.

1759. A Narrative of certain particular Facts which have been misrepresented, relative to the conduct of Mr. Bromfield toward Mr. Aylett, a surgeon and apothecary of Windsor, during their attendance upon Mr. Benwell at Eton. With a letter to Mr. Benwell, and that gentleman's answer. By William Bromfield, surgeon to H.R.H. the Princess Dowager of Wales and St. George's Hospital. Pp. 40. Cr. 8vo. R. & J. Dodsley, London, and C. Layton, Eton. 1759.

[*c.* 1761.] MS. Account of Eton College. By Thomas James. Pp. 162. 12mo.

1766. Designs by Mr. R. Bentley for Six Poems by Mr. T. Gray. Pp. 55. Folio. Dodsley, London. 1766.

1768. The Rebellion at Eton in 1768. By Jeremiah Milles. [A pamphlet; ? title correct.]†

1769. An Account of King's College Chapel in Cambridge ; including a Character of Henry VI., and a Short History of the Foundation of his two colleges, King's and Eton. By Henry Malden, Chapel-Clerk. Illustrated. Pp. 96. Obl. post 8vo. Fletcher & Hodson, Cambridge. 1769.

1770. Sermons on Several Occasions by Thomas Ashton, D.D., Rector of St. Botolph, Bishopsgate, Fellow of Eton College, and late Preacher to the Honourable Society of Lincoln's Inn. Illustrated. Pp. 486. Cr. 8vo. J. Whiston, London. 1770.

1771. An Extract from the Case of the Obligation on the Electors of Eton College to supply all Vacancies in that Society with those who are, or have been Fellows of King's College, Cambridge, so long as Persons properly qualified are to be had within that description. To which are added Two Letters to the Rev. Dr. Morell, in which the cavils of a Writer in the *General Evening Post* and others are considered and refuted. Part I.: Of the Election of Fellows. By a late Fellow of King's College, Cambridge (Dr. Ashton). Pp. 47. Sq. demy 8vo. T. Waller, London. 1771.

1774. Poems. By Dr. Roberts, of Eton College. Pp. 163. Sm. post 8vo. J. Pote, Eton. 1774.

1786. The New Foundling Hospital for Wit, being a Collection of Fugitive Pieces, in Prose and Verse, not in any other Collection. Vol. I. Pp. 323. J. Debrett, Piccadilly. [Contains (p. 7) a poem by Lord Carlisle on his School-fellows at Eton.]

The Poems of Mr. Gray. With notes by Gilbert Wakefield, B.A., late Fellow of Jesus College, Cambridge. Pp. 207. Sm. cr. 8vo. J. Kearsley, London. 1786.

1787. The Microcosm: a Periodical Work. By Gregory Griffin. 40 Numbers. Pp. 455. Post 8vo. C. Knight, Windsor. 1787

1809. The same. Fourth Edition. Inscribed to the Rev. Dr. Davies. 2 vols., 2 ports. Pp. 165, 151. 16mo. Knight, Windsor. 1809.

1825. The same. Fifth Edition. Pp. 295. 12mo. Charles Knight, London. 1825.

[c. 1790.] The Opera of *Il Penseroso* (i.e., the operation of birching). A performance both Vocal and Instrumental, as it is acted at the Royal Theatres of Eton and Westminster. One Coloured Plate: *Circa* 1790. †

1794-6. Scenery and History of the River Thames. By Dr. W. Combe. 2 vols. 76 plates. Imp. 4to. Boydell, London. 1794-6. †

1795. *Musae Etonenses: seu Carminum Delectus nunc primum in lucem editus.* Vols. I., II., III. By G. Herbert. Pp. 336, 276, 64. Demy 8vo. G. Stafford, *Londini.* 1795. Also on Large Paper.

1817. The same. *Editio Altera, aucta.* 3 vols. Pp. 360, 299, 66. Cr. 8vo. T. Ingalton, *Etonae.* 1817.

1796. Poems. By Rev. Henry Rowe. 2 vols. 1796. †

1797. *Alumni Etonenses;* or a Catalogue of the Provosts and Fellows of Eton
College and King's College, Cambridge, from the Foundation in 1443 to
the year 1797; with an Account of their Lives and Preferments collected
from original MSS. and authentic biographical works. By Thomas
Harwood. Pp. 363. Sm. demy 4to. M. Pote, Eton. 1797.

1799. Original Sketch of a Sporting Etonian—in *The Sporting Magazine,* Dec.,
1799. Vol. XV. 8vo. 1799.

1801. Picturesque Views on the River Thames, from its source in Gloucestershire
to the Nore; with Observations on the Public Buildings and other Works
of Art in its Vicinity. By Samuel Ireland. Vols. I., II. Illustrated.
I., pp. 209; II., pp. 258. Sm. roy. 8vo. T. Egerton, Whitehall. 1801.

The Beauties of England and Wales; or Original Delineations, Topogra-
phical, Historical, and descriptive of each County: Bucks, by Edward
Wedlake Brayley and John Britton. Illustrated. Pp. 125. Cr. 8vo.
Hood & Sharpe, London. 1801.

The Poetical Works of George, Lord Lyttelton, with Additions: to which
prefixed, an Account of his Life. Illustrated. [Contains Soliloquy of a
Beauty in the Country (written at Eton).] Pp. 147. Sm. post 8vo.
Caddell & Davies, London. 1801.

1802. The Etonian out of Bounds, and other Poems. By Sir James Lawrence.
Pp. 186. Sm. post 8vo. R. Faulder, London. 1802.

1803. Letter to the Rev. Dr. Goodall, Head Master of Eton School, on the Im-
portance of a Religious Education. Pp. 36. post 8vo. J. Stockdale,
London. 1803.

1806. The Miniature. By Samuel Grildrig, of the College of Eton. Inscribed
by permission to the Rev. Dr. Goodall. Illustrated. 1805. Second
Edition. 2 vols. I., pp. 285; II., pp. 253. 12mo. C. Knight,
Windsor. 1806.

The Translations chiefly from the Greek Anthology, with Tales and Miscellaneous Poems. By Rev. R. Bland and J. H. Merivale. Pp. 233.
Post 8vo. R. Phillips, London. 1806.

1808. The Montem : A Musical Entertainment in two Acts. By the Rev. Henry Rowe, LL.B. Pp. 92. Cr. 8vo. J. Stratford, London. 1808.

1809. *Preces Quotidianae in usum Scholae Collegii Regalis apud Etonam ; quibus adjiciuntur Catechismus cum ordine Confirmationis Graecè et Latinè necnon Articuli Religionis secundum Ecclesiam Anglicanam Latinè redditi.* Pp. 107. 16mo. M. Pote, Windsor. 1809.

1809-10. Poems. I. : Lady Jane Grey, a tale in two books, with miscellaneous poems in English and Latin ; II. : Sir Edgar, a tale in two cantos. with serious translations from the ancients and merry imitations of a modern. By Francis Hodgson, M.A. Pp. 352, 318. Cr. 8vo. J. Mackinlay, London. 1809-10.

1810. Letters from a Nobleman to his Son during the Period of his Education at Eton and Oxford. Vols. I., II. Pp. 328, 359. 12mo. Richard Phillips, London. 1810.
Zastrozzi. By P. B. Shelley, 1810.†

1811. The Thames ; or Graphic Illustrations of Seats, Villas, Public Buildings and Picturesque Scenery on the Banks of that noble river. Engravings by William Bernard Cooke from Drawings by Samuel Owen. 2 vols. Illustrated. Demy 8vo. Vernor, Hood & Sharpe, London. 1811.
The Life of William Waynflete, Bishop of Winchester. By Richard Chandler. Illustrated. Pp. 428. Demy 8vo. White & Cochrane, London. 1811.
Eton College Pony Races—in *The Sporting Magazine*, Aug., 1811 ; vol. XXXVIII., 8vo. 1811. †

1812. A List of Eton College, taken at Election. Pp. 22. Sm. 16mo. Pote & Williams, Eton. 1812.

1813. The History of Windsor and its Neighbourhood. By James Hakewill, Architect. Pp. 359. Royal 4to. Edmund Lloyd, London. 1813.
Gustavus Vasa and other Poems. By W. S. Walker. Pp. 264. Cr. 8vo. Longman & Co., London. 1813.
Magna Britannia, being a concise topographical account of the several Counties of Great Britain. By Daniel and Samuel Lysons. Illustrated.

Vol. I., Part III. : Bucks.   Pp. 279.   Demy 4to.   Cadell & Davies, London.   1813.

1815. The Parent's Assistant.   Vol. VI.   By Maria Edgeworth : Eton Montem. Pp. 224.   32mo.   R. Hunter, London.   1815.

1816. The History of the Colleges of Winchester, Eton and Westminster ; with the Charterhouse, the Schools of St. Paul's, Merchant Taylors, Harrow and Rugby, and the Free School of Christ's Hospital.   Coloured plates. Pp. 366.   Royal 4to.   R. Ackerman, London.   1816.

Report of the Proceedings in the Case of an Appeal preferred by the Provost and Scholars of King's College, Cambridge, against the Provost and Fellows of Eton College to the Lord Bishop of Lincoln, the Visitor of both Societies.   Determined 15th August, 1815.   By Philip Williams, of Lincoln's Inn, Esq., Barrister-at-Law.   Pp. 171.   Cr. 8vo.   J. Butterworth, London.   1816.

1817. The Appeal of King's College against the Fellows of Eton, respecting their holding Ecclesiastical Preferment with their Fellowships.   Preferred A.D. 1814.   Also, The Answer of the latter, and Reply of the former, with other Documents relating to the said Case.   To which are added Remarks critical and explanatory upon Mr. Philip William's Report of the Pleadings in the said case which took place in the Court of Doctor's Commons, 16th and 17th May, 1815.   Pp. 108.   Cr. 8vo.   James Hodson, Cambridge.   1817.

The Dance of Life, a poem by the author of *Dr. Syntax*.   Illustrated with coloured engravings by Thomas Rowlandson.   By William Combe.   Pp. 285.   Long 8vo.   R. Ackermann, London.   1817.

1818. Fourth Report from the Select Committee on the Education of the Lower Orders.   Appendix (*a*) : Documents—Statutes of Eton College.   Pp. 333.   Folio.   House of Commons, 5th June.   1818.

A Concise Description of the Endowed Grammar Schools in England and Wales, ornamented with engravings.   By Nicholas Carlisle.   Vols. I., II.   Pp. 858, 983.   Large demy 8vo.   Baldwin, Cradock & Joy, London.   1818.

1819. Eton College : An Explanation of the various Local Passages and Allusions in the Appeal, etc., of King's College *versus* Eton College. By a Late Scholar. To which are added Remarks upon the Examination of the Provost of Eton College, before the Committee. Pp. 58. Cr. 8vo. Hatchard, London. 1819.

The Windsor Guide: containing a Description of the Town and Castle : the Present State of the Paintings and Curiosities in the Royal Apartments ; an Account of the Monuments, Painted Windows, etc., in St. George's Chapel ; with the Foundation of the Royal College of St. George, and of the Order of the Garter ; also a Description of the Lodges, Parks and Forest. To which is added a brief Account of Eton. A new edition. Pp. 187. 12mo. Knight, Windsor. 1819.

Poetry of *The College Magazine*. Edited by W. Blunt. Pp. 104. Demy 8vo. Knight & Son, Windsor. 1819.

1820-1. The Salt-Bearer : a Periodical Work. By an Etonian. 33 numbers [complete]. May, 1820, to April, 1821. Pp. 380. B. E. Lloyd, London. 1820-1.

The Etonian. Vol. I. : October, 1820, to March, 1821 ; Vol. II. : April. 1821, to August, 1821. Edited by W. Blunt and W. M. Praed. Pp, 400, 446. Cr. 8vo. Knight & Dredge, Windsor. 1821. Second Edition. Vols. I., II. Pp. 412, 488. Obl. cr. 8vo. H. Colburn, London. 1822. Third Edition. Vols. I., II., III. Post 8vo. H. Colburn, London. 1823. Fourth Edition. Vols. I., II., III. Pp. 427, 323, 380. Post 8vo. H. Colburn, London. 1824.

1821. The Student. By Solomon Sap [only one number published]. June, 1821.†

1822. Twenty-five Views on the Thames at Richmond, Eton, Windsor and Oxford. Drawn on stone by W. Westall, A.R.A. Pp. 25. Sq. folio. Rodwell & Martin, London. 1822.

1823. The Eton Montem. By P. A.—in Knight's *Quarterly Magazine*, No 1, June, 1823. Pp. 8. 8vo. C. Knight, London. 1823.

[*c.* 1825.] Theodore and Emma ; or the Italian Bandit. By An Etonian. 12mo. London. †

1825. The Windsor Guide, with a brief account of Eton. A new edition.
Illustrated. Pp. 215. Small post 8vo. C. Knight, Windsor. 1825.

The English Spy. Illustrated. By Bernard Blackmantle [Charles Molloy
Westmacott]. Pp. 77. Demy 8vo. Sherwood & Jones, London.
1825.

CONTENTS: The Five Principle Orders of Eton dames; Election Saturday;
Herbert Stockhore; Life in Eton; Apollo's Visit to Eton; Recollections of an
old Etonian; Eton Montem; Farewell to Eton; My Vale.

1826. *Nugae Canorae quas in Amicorum gratiam imprimi fecit Etonensis.* [By
Rev. George Booth.] Pp. 148. Sq. demy 8vo. *Typis* J. Ham,
Oxoniae. 1826.

The Mirror of Literature, Amusement and Instruction. Illustrated. Vol.
VII. Pp. 428. Cr. 8vo. J. Limbird, London. 1826.

1827. An Excursion to Windsor. By John Evans, LL.D. Pp. 426. Sm. post
8vo. Sherwood, Gilbert & Piper, London. 1827.

Eton and Harrow Match—in the *Annals of Sporting*, Vol. XII. 1827. †

The Eton Miscellany. Vol. I. : June, July ; II. : October, November.
By Bartholomew Bouverie, now of Eton College. Pp. 246, 268. Cr.
8vo. T. Ingalton, Eton. 1827.

Sixty views of Endowed Grammar Schools from original drawings. By J.
C. Buckler ; with letterpress descriptions. 4to. Hurst & Co., London
1827.

The Visitant's Guide to Windsor Castle and its Vicinity.

1828. The same. Fourth Edition. Pp. 156. 12mo. C. Andrews, Windsor.
1828.

[*c.* 1827.] The Triumvirate [only one number published]. *c.* 1827. †

1828. The Oppidan. Two numbers [all published]. Pp. 172. Cr. 8vo. T.
Ingalton, Eton. October, 1828.

Picturesque Tour of the Thames. By W. Westall and S. Owen. 1828. †

An account of the expenses of the two brothers, Mr. Henry and Mr.
William Cavendish, sons of Sir William Cavendish, of Chatsworth,
Knight, at Eton College, beginning 21st October, 2nd Elizabeth, 1560
[from a contemporary Manuscript]—in *The Retrospective Review*, April,
1828. Pp. 7. Cr. 8vo. Baldwin & Cradock, London. 1828.

1829. A Series of Views of the Neighbourhood of Windsor, including the Seats of several of the Nobility and Gentry. Engraved by Landseer, Middiman, W. B. Cooke, G. Cooke, etc., from Drawings taken on the spot by Jas. Hakewill, Architect. Pp. 34. Demy 4to. B. E. Lloyd, London. 1829.

1829-30. Reminiscences of Henry Angelo. With Memoirs of his late Father and Friends. Vols. I. and II. Pp. 510, 558. Demy 8vo. H. Colburn, London. 1828, 1830.

1830-1. Public Schools of England. 1. Eton, 2. Westminster and Eton—in *The Edinburgh Review*, April, 1830, and March, 1831. Pp. 35. Small 8vo. Black, Edinburgh. 1830-1.

1830. Observations on an Article in the Last Number of *The Edinburgh Review*, entitled "Public Schools of England—Eton". By "Etonensis". Pp. 32. Cr. 8vo. Ridgway, London. 1830.

1831. Reminiscences of Eton. By An Etonian. Pp. 152. Cr. 8vo. J. Hackman, Chichester. 1831.
Excerpta Historica: or, illustrations of English History. Pp. 444. Sm. roy. 8vo. S. Bentley, London. 1831.

1831-47. History of Buckinghamshire. By G. Lipscombe. [4 vols.] Vol. IV., section on "Eton".†

1832. Montem : a Poem. By An Etonian. Pp. 36. Cr. 8vo. T. Ingalton, Eton. 1832.

1832. The Year-Book of Daily Recreation and Information. By William Hone. Illustrated. Pp. 826. Demy 8vo. W. Tegg, Cheapside. 1832.

1832. The Eton College Magazine. Edited by J. Wickens. June-November, 1832. 8 numbers [all published]. Pp. 309. Sm. demy 8vo. Ingalton Eton, 1832.
Farewell to Montem. By W. Selwyn. 1832.†
Eton School List in *The Gentleman's Magazine*, Jan., 1832. 8vo.†
Perseus Redivivus. A Satire. 1832.†
The Pilgrim, and other Poems. Hatchard, Piccadilly. 1832.†

1833. The Kaleidoscope: a Periodical conducted by Eton Boys : 28th January
to 24th June, 1833. 9 numbers. Pp. 348. Cr. 8vo. T. Ingalton,
Eton. 1833.

1834. Eton School: Education in England—in *The Quarterly Review*, August,
1834. Pp. 50. Demy 8vo. Murray, London. 1834.

Some Remarks on the Present Studies and Management of Eton School.
By A Parent. The same. Second Edition. Pp. 33. Post 8vo. J.
Ridgway, London. 1834. A Few Words in reply to the above. By
" Etonensis ". Pp. 20. Post 8vo. J. Hatchard & Son, London. 1834.

The Eton System of Education Vindicated and its Capabilities of Improve-
ment Considered ; in reply to some recent publications. 8vo. Pp. 30.
Rivington, London. 1834.†

The Eton Abuses Considered in a Letter addressed to the author of
" Some Remarks on the Present Studies and Management of Eton
School". Second Edition. Pp. 36. Cr. 8vo. Ridgway, London. 1834.

1835. The Youth's *Cornucopia*. Second Edition. Illustrated. Pp. 292. 12mo.
John Chidley, London. 1835.

Montem Lists: from 1773 to 1834, inclusive. Pp. 63. Obl. cr. 8vo. T.
Ingalton, Eton. 1835.

Evidence on behalf of Eton College in opposition to the G. W. Railway
Bill. Pp. 62. Post 8vo. Baynes & Harris, London. 1835.

1836. A List of Eton College taken at Election. Pp. 20. Sq. post 8vo. E.
Williams, Eton. 1836.

Eton Revisited : in August, 1836. By μ—in Colburn's *New Monthly
Magazine*, Vol. XLVIII., Part III. 1836. Pp. 9. Cr. 8vo. H.
Colburn, London. 1836.

1837. Poems. By T. W. Allies (First Newcastle Scholar, 1827). Pp. 193. Sm.
12mo. Talboys, Oxford. 1837.

Self-Formation, or the History of an Individual Mind ; intended as a Guide
for the Intellect through Difficulties to Success. By a Fellow of a
College [Capel Loft]. Vols. I., II. Pp. 285, 271. Post 8vo. C.
Knight, London. 1837.

1838. Poems. By John Moultrie. Vol. I. Pp. 359. 12mo. W. Pickering, London. 1838.

The Eton Classical Casket. By M. H. Pp. 33. Post 8vo. Ingalton & Son, Eton. 1838.

1839. *Fasciculus Carminum Stylo Lucretiano Scriptorum auctoribus doctis quibusdam viris in sinu Regiæ Scholæ Etonensis Musarum Disciplina olim institutis.* Pp. 52. Cr. 8vo. E. P. Williams, Eton. 1839.

Il Trifoglio ovvero scherzi metrici d'un Inglese : non publicati, ma presentati a quei pochi amici, cui piacque " meas esse aliquid putare nugas". [E. C. Hawtrey.] Pp. 89. Cr. 8vo. Wertheimer, Londra, 1839.

1840. Eton Addresses : 1831-1836. Pp. 56. Cr. 8vo. [Also on Large Paper. T. Ingalton & Son, Eton. 1840.

The Thames and its Tributaries, or Rambles among the Rivers. By Charles Mackay. Illustrated. Vols. I., II. Pp. 400, 412. Cr. 8vo. R. Bentley, London. 1840.

Windsor Castle and its Environs ; including Eton College. By Leitch Ritchie. Illustrated. Royal 8vo. Longmans, London. 1840. 1848. The same. Second Edition, with Additions by Edward Jesse. Pp. 312. Demy 8vo. H. G. Bohn, London. 1848.

Sale Catalogue of Dr. Goodall's Library. Pp. 82. Cr. 8vo. Leigh & Sotheby, London. 1840.

Extracts from the Statutes of Eton College, with Remarks. By an Etonian, a Member of the Inner Temple—in *The Morning Chronicle,* 22nd April, 1840. Pp. 20. Sm. 16mo. R. Oxley, Windsor. 1840.

A Day at Eton. By E. Jesse—in Bentley's *Miscellany,* 12th May, 1840, Pp. 6. Demy 8vo. Bentley, London. 1840.

Primitiæ et Reliquiæ. By the Marquis of Wellesley. Pp. 90. Sm. demy 8vo. G. Nichol, London. 1840.

Eton. Newcastle Scholarship—in *The Educational Magazine,* edited by Rev. F. D. Maurice. New Series. Vol. I. May, 1840. Pp. 5. Cr. 8vo. Darton & Clark, London. 1840.

1841. The Etonian and Geoffrey Selwood. By Charlotte Adams. 18mo. Booth, London. 1841.†

Eton Sketched by " Quis ".   4to.   Baxter, Oxford.   1841.†

A Letter to His Royal Highness Prince Albert on his Establishment of an
  Annual Prize at Eton College for the Encouragement of Modern
  Literature.   By an Etonian.

The same. Second Edition.   Pp. 19.   Cr. 8vo.   Ridgway, London.   1841.

A Summer Day at Windsor and a Visit to Eton.   By Edward Jeose.
  Illustrated.   Pp. 151.   12mo.   John Murray, London.   1841.

The same.   A New Edition.   Pp. 92.   Sm. 12mo.   John Murray, London.
  1843.

Rules of the Etonian Club established in Oxford, 24th April, 1839.   Pp.
  15.   Obl. 12mo.   J. Munday, Oxford.   1841.

1842.   The Works of Roger Hutchinson, Fellow of St. John's College, Cambridge,
  and afterwards of Eton Coll., A.D. 1550.   Edited for the Parker Society
  by John Bruce, Esq.   Pp. 366.   8vo.   University Press, Cambridge.
  1842.

The Eton Bureau.   7 numbers [all published].   Pp. 336.   Ingalton &
  Son, Eton.   1842.

Recollections of Eton.   By An Etonian—in the *New Monthly Magazine and
  Humorist*, edited by Thomas Hood.   Pp. 45.   Cr. 8vo.   H. Colburn,
  London.   1842.

The Eton Calendar.   1842.   The same.   Second Edition.   Pp. 24.   Sm.
  16mo.   E. P. Williams, Eton.   1842.

Report of the State of the Drainage of Eton College and Eton, with
  Suggested Improvements, and on the Occasional Floods from the
  River Thames, in a Letter addressed to the Rev. Dr. Hawtrey, Head-
  Master of Eton College.   By John Roe, A.T.C.E.   Pp. 16.   Cr. 8vo.
  R. Spencer, London.   1842.

New Zealand : a poem.   Dedicated to the Rev. E. Coleridge, by An Old
  Etonian.   Pp. 30.   Obl. 12mo.   L. & G. Seeley, London.   1842.

1843.   Poems: The Dream of Life, Lays of the English Church.   By John
  Moultrie.   Vol. II.   Pp. 368.   12mo.   W. Pickering, London.   1843.

Lighter Hours: a Series of Poems.   By An Etonian.   Pp. 155.   12mo.
  Ingalton & Son, Eton.   1843.

A Few Words to the Provost of Eton (F. Hodgson).   Upon certain late proceedings of his in the Religious Government of Eton College. By An Etonian. 1843.†

1844. Memorials of Eton College. By C. W. Radcliffe. Pp. 48 ; lithographs. Folio. T. Ingalton, Eton. 1844.

Eton Scenes and Eton Men. By Robert Armitage, author of "Doctor Hookwell"—in Bentley's *Miscellany*, July, August, November, 1844. Pp. 29. Demy 8vo. Bentley, London. 1844.

Coningsby, or the New Generation. By the Right Hon. B. Disraeli [later Earl of Beaconsfield] 1844. New Edition. Pp. 477. Post 8vo. Longmans, Green & Co., London. 1870.

1845. The Art of Losing one's Remove: a Treatise : being a Preparation to the Art of Pluck : to which is added Fragments from the Trial Papers. By "Scriblerus Etonensis". Pp. 23. Obl. 12mo. Ingalton & Son, Eton. [1845.]

1846. Euornos. By An Old Etonian. Pp. 103. 16mo. E. P. Williams, Eton. 1846.

The Legacy of an Etonian. Edited by "Robert Nolands," Sole Executor. Pp. 181. Cr. 8vo. Macmillan & Barclay, Cambridge. 1846.

The Confessions of an Etonian. By I. E. M. Pp. 150. Cr. 8vo. Saunders & Otley, London. 1846.

Lectures on the Church Catechism, delivered in Eton College Chapel. By E. C. Hawtrey. Pp. 235. 12mo. C. H. Lambert, Paris. 1846. Not published.

Random Recollections of an Eton Life. By "Amator Etonæ". Dedicated *Lectori Studioso*. Pp. 23. Sm. 12mo. Simpkin & Marshall, London. 1846.

Memoirs and Correspondence of the Most Noble Richard, Marquess Wellesley. By Robert Rouiere Pearce. Illustrated. 3 vols. Pp. 431, 460, 456. 8vo. R. Bentley, London. 1846.

1847. Favourite Haunts and Rural Studies ; including Visits to Spots of Interest in the Vicinity of Windsor and Eton. By Edward Jesse. Illustrated. Pp. 365. Post 8vo. John Murray, London. 1847.

The Last Days of Eton Montem. By W. D. (From Sharpe's *London Magazine*, 7th August, 1847). Pp. 3. Sm. roy. 8vo. T. B. Sharpe, London. 1847.

Ralph Roister Doister, a Comedy [1566] by Nicholas Udall; and The Tragedy of Gorboduc [1561] by Thomas Norton and Thomas Sackville, with Introductory Memoirs. Edited by William Durrant Cooper, F.S.A. Pp. 160. Demy 8vo. Shakespeare Society, London. 1847.

Fagging: Is it hopelessly inseparable from the discipline of a Public School? Cr. 8vo. Pp. 28. Hatchard, London. 1847.†

Nugæ Etonenses: I. A Letter from W. Mum, Esq., to his brother, Jack, now drinking the Cheltenham waters, but late of the Embassy to Cochin China; II. Jack Mum's Experiences, edited by his Brother. (1) A fairy tale of Windsor; (2) The Lay of the Block. Pp. 7, 9. Crown 8vo. Brown, Windsor. 1847.

Life of P. B. Shelley. By Thomas Medwin. 2 vols. 1847.

1847-8. The Eton School Magazine, consisting of Original Papers of a Miscellaneous Literary Character in Prose and Verse, the entire production of Eton Boys of the Present Day. 6 numbers [complete]. Pp. 240. Demy 8vo. Williams, Eton. 1847-8.

1848. Some Account of the Foundation of Eton College and of the Past and Present Condition of the School. With Appendix. By [Sir] E[dward] S. Creasy. Pp. 132. Post 8vo. Longmans, London. 1848.

The Life of Richard Allestree, Provost of Eton. By Bishop Fell. 32mo. J. Masters, London. 1848.†

Eton College—in *The Prospective Review*, Vol. IV., No. 15, July, 1848. Pp. 13. Demy 8vo. John Chapman, London. 1848.

Tick: Memories of an old Eton Boy. By Charles Rowcroft. (From *The New Monthly Magazine*, 1848.) Pp. 165. Cr. 8vo. Chapman & Hall, London. 1848.

1847-9. Rambles by Rivers: The Thames. By James Thorne. Vols. I., II. Illustrated. Pp. 223. 240. 32mo. Cox, London. 1847-9.

1849. Sermons and Lectures delivered in Eton College Chapel in the years 1848-9. By E. C. Hawtrey. [Not published.] Pp. 114. 12mo. E. P. Williams, Eton. 1849.

1850. The Ancient Laws of the Fifteenth Century for King's College, Cambridge, and for the Public School of Eton College. Collected by James Heywood, M.P., and Thomas Wright, M.A. Pp. 640. Demy 8vo. Longmans, London. 1850.

Memoirs of Celebrated Etonians. By Sir Edward Creasy. Roy. 8vo. 1850. New Edition, with Illustrations. Pp. 640. Cr. 8vo. Chatto & Windus, London. 1876.

[?] A Brief Memoir of an Eton Boy. ? 1850. The same. Second Edition. Pp. 62. Sq. 32mo. Seeley, London. 1851.

[c. 1850.] Pamphlet on Examination of Members of King's College, Cambridge, for Degrees ; with Appendix containing the Narrative of Mr. Reynold's [King's, 1689], Fellow of Eton and Canon of Exeter.†

1851. Our Heartless Policy : dedicated to the high-minded and reflecting of all nations at the approaching Exhibition. By An Etonian. Pp. 72. Sm. 8vo. J. Ridgway, London. 1851.

Eton Address to the Queen. Spoken by E. D. Stone. 1851.†

1852. Confessions of an Etonian. By Charles Rowcroft. 3 vols. Pp. 325, 323, 298. Post 8vo. Colburn, London. 1852.

A Dream : a Ballad supposed to have been written about the Year Eighteen hundred and fifty-two. By " Etonensis " [= J. H. Arkwright]. Pp. 15. 12mo. R. Oxley, Windsor. 1852.

Gray's Poetical Works, English and Latin. Illustrated. With Introductory Stanzas by the Rev. John Moultrie, and an Original Life of Gray by the Rev. John Mitford. Eton Illustrated (Third) Edition. Pp. 142. Demy 8vo. E. P. Williams, Eton. 1852.

A Short Account of Eton Montem, explanatory of Mr. Evans' Engravings of that Ceremony. By An Etonian. Pp. 24. Obl. 12mo. J. Hogarth, London. 1852.

Addresses delivered by Thackeray and Mathias, K.S., in the Upper School on the Visit of His Royal Highness Prince Albert to the Eton Speeches. Pp. 8. Sm. post 8vo. 4th June, 1852.

William of Wykeham and his Colleges. By Mackenzie E. Walcott. Illustrated. Pp. xvi., 473. Demy 8vo. D. Nutt, Winchester. 1852.

The Poetical Remains of William Sidney Walker. Edited, with a
memoir of the author, by the Rev. J. Moultrie. Pp. 200. 12mo. J.
W. Parker, London. 1852.

Waking Thoughts after "A Dream". For private circulation. Pp. 8.
Obl. 12mo. E. P. Williams, Eton. A Reply (τὸ ἄληθες). By J. H.
Arkwright. Pp. 4. 12mo. T. Ingalton Drake. 1852.

1853. A Picturesque Tour of the River Thames in its Western Course. By John
Fisher Murray. Illustrated. Pp. 356. Demy 8vo. H. G. Bohn,
London. 1853.

The Alphabet Annotated for Youth and Adults, in Doggerel Verse, by an
Old Etonian. Engravings by G. W. Terry. 4to. 15s. Ackermann,
London. 1853.

1853-62. Sale Catalogues of Dr. Hawtrey's Library. 2 vols. Pp. 104, 192. Cr.
8vo. Leigh, Sotheby & Wilkinson, London. 1853-62 [See also 1840.]

1854. Poems: Altars, Hearths and Graves. By John Moultrie. Vol. III. Pp.
269. 12mo. Hamilton, Adams & Co., London. 1854.

The Life and Correspondence of Charles, Lord Metcalfe, late Governor-
General of India, Governor of Jamaica, and Governor-General of
Canada; from Unpublished Letters and Journals preserved by himself,
his family, and his friends. By John William Kaye. Vols. I., II. Pp.
516, 654. Demy 8vo. R. Bentley, London. 1854.

Eton Address to the Prince Consort and the King of Portugal. Spoken
by Oscar Browning. 1854.†

The Vale of an Old Etonian : Election 1854 : a Poem. Pp. 7. Williams,
Eton.†

[c. 1854.] Eton and Oxford : A few familiar scenes sketched from recollection
after an interval of several years, and dedicated by permission to the
Earl of Darnley by a contemporary [Rev. G. R. Winter]. 12 Eton
plates. Two Series. Ryman, Oxford, n.d.†

Miseries of Eton. By A. H. A. Morton.†

1856. The Song of Floggawaya. Pp. ii., 10. 16mo. C. S. Burbige, London.
1856.†

A Sermon preached in Eton College Chapel on Sunday, 27th July, by John, Lord Bishop of Lincoln [Jackson], Visitor of the College. Pp. 20. Cr. 8vo. E. P. Williams, Eton. 1856. Privately printed.

Six Sermons preached in Eton College Chapel in 1855-6. By E. C. Haw. trey [not published]. Pp. 92. 12mo. E. P. Williams, Eton. 1856.

Poets and Statesmen, their Homes and Memorials in the Neighbourhood of Windsor and Eton. By William Dowling. Illustrated by E. and C. W. Radclyffe. Demy 8vo. 1856. The same. New Edition. Pp. 312. Demy 8vo. E. P. Williams, Eton. 1856. The same. New Edition. Griffin, London. 1862.

1856-69. *Musæ Etonenses sive Carminum Etonæ Conditorum Delectus.* Series Nova. Tom. I., fasc. i., 1856; fasc. ii., 1862. Tom. II., 1869. Ricardus Okes. Pp. 100, 192, 141. Demy 8vo. E. P. Williams, Eton. 1856-69.

1857. *Registrum Regale.* Edited by G. J. Dupuis. 1857. †
A Visit to Eton. (From *Fraser's Magazine.* Vol. LVI. 1857.)

1858. Annals of Windsor, with an account of Eton. By Robert Richard Tighe and James Edward Davis. 2 vols. Maps and Illustrations. Pp. 705, 752. Royal 8vo. Longmans, London. 1858.
A Sermon preached in Eton College Chapel on Election Sunday, 24th July, by the Venerable C. J. Abraham, B.D., Archdeacon of Waitemata, New Zealand. Pp. 16. 12mo. E. P. Williams, Eton. 1858.
Eton and Winchester Election Trial Verses. By J. C. Evans. 1858.†

1858-60. Shelley. By T. L. Peacock—in *Fraser's Magazine.* Vol. LVII. June, 1858. Pp. 643-59. LXVI., January, 1860. Pp. 92-109. March, 1860. Pp. 301-19.

1858-77. Ionica. Parts I., II. By W. Johnson [=W. Cory; New Edition. 1891, *infra*]. Pp. 166. 12mo. Smith & Elder, London and Cambridge University Press. 1858-77.

1859. The Portico: Public School Magazine. Vols. I., II. 18 numbers [all published]. Pp. 398. Large cr. 8vo. Whittaker, London. 1859.

Eton Montem. By Charles Knight. "Once upon a Time." Pp. 7.
12mo. Murray, London. 1859.

A Magazine Squib. 1859.†

Some Account of the Exhibitions and Scholarships for Superannuated and
other Eton Scholars, with the Names of the Present Holders, etc. Pp.
16. Sm. 16mo. Williams, Eton. Election, 1859.

Porticus Etonensis: supported entirely by Present Etonians. Nos. I., II.
[all published]. Pp. 32. Cr. 8vo. Ingalton & Drake, Eton. 1859.

A Critique on the *Eton Observer.* 1859.†

1859-60. The Eton Observer. 10 numbers.

1859-62. The Eton Register: Boating, Cricketing, Football, Running, Shooting.
Pp. 257. Cr. 8vo. Ingalton & Drake, Eton. 1859-62.

1860. A List of the Eton College Volunteer Corps. Pp. 8. Sm. 16mo.
Williams, Eton. July, 1860.

Etonalia: (1) *De Naturâ Deorum;* (2) "The Bobby"; (3) *Vale Etona.*
Pp. 16. Sm. 8vo. W. S. Johnson, London. 1860.

The Comic Eton Latin Grammar. With numerous Illustrations by John
Leech. 1860.

Wild Oates and Dead Leaves. By Albert Smith. Chapman & Hall,
London. Pp. 156. 12mo. Ward & Lock, London. 1860.

Anti-paterfamilias' Views on Eton. By a Present Etonian. Pp. 13. Obl.
cr. 8vo. Ingalton & Drake, Eton. 1860.

A Public School Education : a Lecture delivered at the Athenæum,
Tiverton, 1860. By Sir John T. Coleridge. John Murray, London.
1860. The same. Second and Third Editions. Pp. 96. 12mo. John
Murray, London. 1860, 1861.

1860-1. The Phœnix. Conducted by Present Etonians. 1st October, 1860, to
1st March, 1861. 5 numbers [complete]. Pp. 124. Cr. 8vo. E. P.
Williams, Eton. 1860-1.

1860-4. Letters from Paterfamilias to the *Cornhill Magazine*—i., May, 1860; ii.,
December, 1860; iii., March, 1861; iv., July, 1864. Pp. 46. Demy
8vo. Smith & Elder, London. 1860-4. [Some points of the Eton
Report.]

1861. The Public School Matches: a Correct Account of all the Matches of which the Scores are in existence, played between the Schools of Eton, Harrow, and Winchester from 1805 to the present year. Pp. 93. 16mo. F. Lillywhite, Kennington Oval. 1861.

Eton: Review of Sir J. Coleridge's Lecture and W. Johnson's "Eton Reform"—in *The Westminster Review*, April, 1861. Pp. 26. Cr. 8vo. Manwaring, London. 1861.

Eton Reform. Part I., II. By William Johnson [later adopted surname Cory]. Pp. 34, 43. Cr. 8vo. Longmans, London. 1861.

Eton College: Review of Creasy's "Foundation" [1848], Sir J. Coleridge's Lecture [1860], and W. Johnson's "Eton Reform" [1861]—in *The Edinburgh Review*, April, 1861. Pp. 40. Demy 8vo. A. & C. Black, Edinburgh. 1861.

Our Nicknames at Playingfield College. By P. S. F.—in *Once a Week*, 4th May, 1861. Pp. 8. Sm. 8vo. Bradbury & Evans, London. 1861.

Eton. By Another Paterfamilias. Pp. 14. Cr. 8vo. E. P. Williams, Eton. 1861.

Guide to Eton. Eton Alphabet. Eton Block. Eton Glossary. Pp. 71. 12mo. Whittaker, London. 1861.

Thoughts on Eton, suggested by Sir John Coleridge's Speech at Tiverton. By An Etonian. Pp. 35. 12mo. Rivingtons, London. 1861.

Eton—in *Macmillan's Magazine*, February, 1861. Pp. 9. 8vo. Macmillan & Co., London. 1861.

1862. The Kean Banquet, Wednesday, 20th July, 1859, His Grace the Duke of Newcastle in the Chair: and The Kean Testimonial Presentation, Saturday, 22nd March, 1862, Right Hon. W. E. Gladstone, M.P. (Chancellor of the Exchequer) in the Chair. Pp. 48. Post 8vo. W. Brettell, London. 1862.

Windsor: A History and Description of the Castle and Town. By the Rev. John Stoughton. Illustrated. Pp. 244. 12mo. Ward & Co., London. 1862.

1863. A List of the Eton College Rifle Corps. Taken March. Pp. 10. 12mo. Ingalton & Drake, Eton. 1863.

Etonensia : conducted by Etonians. Parts I., II. Pp. 36, 32. Cr. 8vo. Ingalton & Drake, Eton. 1863.

Breakfast in Bed, or Philosophy between the Sheets. By George Augustus Sala. Pp. 334. Post 8vo. John Maxwell, London. 1863. The same. New Edition. 12mo. John Maxwell, London. 1864.

The Eton Boys. By F. G. Illustrated—in *The Boy's Own Volume,* December, 1863. Pp. 6. Cr. 8vo. Beeton, London. 1863.

A Sermon preached in Eton College Chapel on Election Sunday, 26th July, 1863, by the Rev. T. T. Carter, Rector of Clewer. Williams, Eton. 1863.†

1863-95. Eton College Chronicle. Nos. 1-14. Pp. 56. Royal 4to. E. P. Williams, Eton. 1863. Nos. 15-33 (1864), pp. 76 ; 35-50 (1865), pp. 68 ; 51-71 (1866), pp. 84 ; 72-93 (1867), pp. 90 ; 94-112 (1868), pp. 76 ; 113-130 (1869), pp. 72 ; 131-148 (1870), pp. 72 ; 149-165 (1871)' pp. 68 ; 166-183 (1872), pp. 72 ; 184-199 (1873), pp. 64 ; 200-216 (1874), pp. 68 ; 217-234 (1875), pp. 72 ; 235-252 (1876), pp. 68,; 253-269 (1877), pp. 68 ; 270-288 (1878), pp. 76 ; 289-305 (1879), pp. 68 ; 306-323 (1880), pp. 72 ; 324-340 (1881), pp. 68 ; 341-357 (1882), pp. 68 ; 358-374 (1883), pp. 68 ; 375-395 (1884), pp. 84 ; 397-416 (1885), pp. 88 ; 418-436 (1886), pp. 76 ; 437-460 (1887), pp. 96 ; 461-487 (1888), pp. 198 ; 488-514 (1889), pp. 108 ; 515-542 (1890), pp. 110 ; 543-572 (1891), pp. 122 ; 573-604 (1892), pp. 128 ; 605-639 (1893), pp. 140 ; 640-672 (1894), pp. 132 ; 673-712 (1895), pp. 160 ; 713-748 (1896), pp. 144 ; 749-784 (1897), pp. 181. Royal 4to. Williams, Eton, 1863-76. 1877-81, W. Lowman, Eton. 1882-97, Ingalton Drake, Eton.

1863-4. The Early Days of an M. F. H.—in *Baily's Magazine.* Vols. VII., VIII. Pp. 138. Sm. 8vo. A. H. Baily, London. 1863-4.

1864. Passages of a Working Life during Half a Century ; with a Prelude of Early Reminiscences. By Charles Knight. Vols. I.-III. Pp. 346, 336, 344. Post 8vo. Bradbury & Evans, London. 1864.

The Poems of Winthrop Mackworth Praed. With a Memoir by the Rev. Derwent Coleridge. 2 vols. Pp. 397, 439. 12mo. Moxon, London. 1864.

Football at Rugby, Eton and Harrow. By J. D. C.—in *London Society*, Vol. V., March, 1864. Pp. 10. Cr. 8vo. 9 St. Bride's Avenue, London, E.C. 1864.

Report of Her Majesty's Commissioners appointed to inquire into the Revenues and Management of certain Colleges and Schools, and the Studies pursued and Instruction given therein. 4 vols. Pp. 338, 604, 534, 436. Eton Index, pp. 41 [MS.]. Folio. Eyre & Spottiswoode, London. 1864. Vol. I., Report; Vol. II., Appendix; Vols. III., IV., Evidence.

On the Report of the Commissioners appointed to inquire into the Condition of the Principal Public Schools, etc. By Dr. W. B. Hodgson. 1864.†

Eton School Days, or Recollections of an Etonian. By Bracebridge Hemyng. Pp. 316. Sm. 8vo. Ward, Lock & Tyler, London. 1864. New Edition. 12mo. Ward, Lock & Tyler, London. 1870.

The Public School Matches of 1864—in *Baily's Magazine*, August, 1864. Pp. 10. Cr. 8vo. A. H. Baily, London. 1864.

The Public Schools Report: Eton—in *Blackwood's Magazine*, June, 1864. Pp. 25. Demy 8vo. Blackwood, Edinburgh. 1864.

Eton and Harrow: or Pearls before the Swine. By the Gentleman in Black—in *Baily's Magazine*, August, 1864. Pp. 8. Cr. 8vo. A. H. Baily, London. 1864.

Eton Reform—in *The* [old] *National Review*, January, 1864. Pp. 22. 8vo.†

Report of the Public Schools Commission—in *The* [old] *National Review*, November, 1864. Pp. 40. 8vo.†

Poland. In Verse. By an Etonian. 12mo. Pp. 15. Macmillan, London. 1864.†

1865. The Public Schools Calendar. Edited by a Graduate of the University of Oxford. First Issue. Pp. 540. 12mo. Rivingtons, London. 1865.

A Few Words with the Eton Reformers. With a List of the Newcastle Select. By Henry Brandreth, Fellow of Trinity College, Cambridge. Pp. 48. Cr. 8vo. Spottiswoode, London. 1865.

The Eton Scrap Book: consisting of Original Papers of a Miscellaneous Literary Character in Prose and Verse; the entire production of

Etonians. 7 numbers [all published], May to December, 1865. Pp. 144. Cr. 8vo. E. P. Williams, Eton. 1864.

The Great Schools of England : An Account of the Foundation, Endowments and Discipline of the Chief Seminaries of Learning in England. By Howard Staunton. Illustrated. Pp. 517. Cr. 8vo. Sampson Low, London. 1865.

Etoniana, Ancient and Modern ; being Notes of the History and Traditions of Eton College. Republished from *Blackwood's Magazine*, with Additions. By the Rev. W. L. Collins. Pp. 238. 12mo. Blackwood, London. 1865.

Butler Burke at Eton. By Bracebridge Hemyng. Pp. 315. Post 8vo. John Maxwell & Co., London. 1865.

Remarks upon the Report of the Public Schools Commission. Pp. 46. Cr. 8vo. For Private Circulation. 1865.

Promotion at Eton. By W. K. Wilson. Pp. 32. Cr. 8vo. Crossley, Rugby. For Private Circulation only. 1865.

Report from the Select Committee of the House of Lords on the Public Schools Bill (H. L.) ; together with the Proceedings of the Committee, Minutes of Evidence, Appendix and Index. Pp. 340. Folio. Eyre & Spottiswoode, London. 5th July, 1865.

Eton as it is. By " Quis "—in *The Victoria Magazine*, Dec., 1864, Jan., 1865. Vol. IV. Nos. 19-21. 8vo. Ward & Lock, London. 1865.†

1866.   Eton Sixty Years Since—in *Chambers's Journal*, September, 1866. Pp. 8. Royal 8vo. W. & R. Chambers, Edinburgh. 1866.

The Annals of Eton. (From *Chambers's Journal*, 1866.) Pp. 5. Royal 8vo. W. & R. Chambers, Edinburgh. 1866.

The Thames, Illustrated by Photographs: Richmond to Cliefden. Pp. 30. Sq. post 8vo. Marion, London. 1866.

1867.   Eton—in *Macmillan's Magazine*, March, 1867. Pp. 13. Demy 8vo. Macmillan, London. 1867.

Work First or Play First : a few thoughts for the consideration of Eton Masters. Pp. 16. Cr. 8vo. 1867.

Reminiscences of a French Eton. By the Rev. Stephen Hawtrey. The same. Second Edition. Pp. 79. Sm. post 8vo. Mary S. Rickerby, London. 1867.

1867-72. The Adventurer: conducted by Present Etonians. 29 numbers (complete). 4 vols. Pp. 480, 480, 480, 240. Cr. 8vo. E. P. Williams, Eton. 1867-72.

1868. Eton—in The British Quarterly Review, January, 1868. Pp. 36. Demy 8vo. Hodder & Stoughton, London. 1868.

Eton: Things Old and New. By an old K. S. Pp. 16. Cr. 8vo. Longmans, Green & Co., London. 1868.

The Birds of Berkshire and Buckinghamshire: a Contribution to the Natural History of the Two Counties. By A. W. M. Clark Kennedy, "An Eton Boy". Illustrated. Pp. 232. Post 8vo. Ingalton & Drake, Eton. 1868.

The Life of James Lonsdale, Bishop of Lichfield; with some of his Writings. Edited by Edmund Beckett Denison. Illustrated. Pp. 355. Post 8vo. J. Murray, London. 1868.

1869. Dr. Verney's Eton Days—in London Society. Vol. XV., June, 1869. Pp. 16. Demy 8vo. 217 Piccadilly, London. 1869.

Two Lectures on English History: I.: Henry VIII. and Edward VI., by G. E. Marindin; II.: Mary and Elizabeth, by Rev. E. Hale. Pp. 44. Cr. 8vo. E. P. Williams, Eton. 1869.

1870. The Tutorial System at Eton. By John Walford, M.A. (From The Month, April, 1870.) Pp. 13. Demy 8vo. Burns & Oates, London. 1870.

Recollections of Eton. By An Etonian. Illustrated by Sydney P. Hall. Pp. 362. Cr. 8vo. Chapman & Hall, London. 1870.

1871. Eton as it is, or Another Side of the Question. By An Etonian. Pp. 12. 16mo. E. P. Williams, Eton. 1871.

Sun Pictures of Eton College, with brief descriptive matter by John Harrington. Ingalton Drake, Eton. 1871. †

"Collegers v. Oppidans": a Reminiscence of Eton Life—in The Cornhill Magazine, December, 1871. Pp. 30. 8vo. Smith & Elder, London. 1871.

Look Before You Leap: or, Another Account of the Fight at Dame Europa's School. By A Present Etonian. Pp. 16. E. P. Williams, Eton. 1871.

A Plea for All Sides: or, The Views of a *real* Neutral concerning the Row at Dame Europa's School. By An Etonian. Pp. 9. 12mo. Ingalton Drake, Eton. 1871.

1872. Something about Eton. By An Old Etonian: W. D. R—in *Lippincott's Magazine*, October, 1872. Pp. 8. 8vo. Lippincott, Philadelphia. 1872.

Official Correspondence of Thomas Bekynton, Secretary to King Henry VI. and Bishop of Bath and Wells. Rolls Series. 2 vols. Pp. ccxi., 295, 432. Obl. 8vo. Longmans, London. 1872.

(1) The Effect of Civilisation upon Poetry. By E. K. Corrie. (2) The Poetry of the Period. By J. E. C. Welldon. Papers read before the Eton Literary and Scientific Society. Pp. 28. Obl. 12mo. Williams & Son, Eton. 1872.

The Works of John Hookham Frere, in Verse and Prose; with a memoir by his nephews, W. E. and Sir Bartle Frere. 2 vols. Pp. ccxcv., 322; iv., 496. Demy 8vo. Pickering, London. New Edition, 1872. 3 vols.

1873. Amadeus and Other Poems. By Alfred Wyatt-Edgell. Pp. 118. Cr. 8vo. Smith & Elder, London. 1873.

A Sermon preached in Eton College Chapel. By H. M. Birch, B.D., On Election Sunday. Pp. 16. Sm. 8vo. Williams & Son, Eton. 1873.

The Development of Gothic Architecture in England. By R. C. Reade. A paper read before the Eton Literary and Scientific Society. Illustrated. Pp. 30. Obl. 12mo. Williams & Son, Eton. 1873.

(1) The Revelations of the Subterranean World concerning Prehistoric Man; (2) Glaciers. By A. C. Cole. Papers read before the Eton Literary and Scientific Society. Pp. 26. Obl. 12mo. Williams & Son, Eton. 1873.

1874. The Life and Letters of Rowland Williams, D.D. With Extracts from his Note-Books. Edited by his Wife. 2 vols. Pp. 416, 416. Post 8vo. H. S. King, London. 1874.

The Phœnix. [One number.] Pp. 24. 8vo. Williams, Eton. 1874.

Historical MSS. Commission : Fourth Report, Part I. : Archbishoɔ Laud's Visitation of Eton College. Pp. 12. Sm. Folio. Eyre & Spottswoode, London. 1874.

Sketches of Eton : Etchings and Vignettes by Richard S. Chattock, and Descriptive Notes by W. Wightman Wood. Pp. 58. Imp. 8vo. Seeley, Jackson & Halliday. London. 1874.

Public Schools Commission : Reports and Private Papers. Pp. 304. Sm. Folio. Eyre & Spottiswoode. 1874.

My Time and what I've done with it : an autobiography. By F. C. Burnand. Illustrated. Pp. 447. Post 8vo. Burns & Oates. London. 1874. [Since reprinted by Bradbury & Agnew.]

[c. 1874.] Wright's Guide to Eton College. Pp. 31. Sm. 8vo. Wright Bros., Windsor. c. 1874.

1875. The Art of Swimming in the Eton Style. By Sergeant Leahy. Preface by Mrs. Oliphant. Illustrated by F. Tarver. Edited by Two Etonians [C. F. M. M. and G. A. M.]. Pp. 116. Sm. 8vo. Macmillan, London. 1875.

The Salt-Hill Papers, or *Vindiciæ Etonenses.* By Two Etonians. Pp. 12. Cr. 8vo. Williams. Eton College. 4th June, 1875.

The Sugar-Loaf Papers. By Three Etonians— Brown, Jones and Robinson. Pp. 22. Cr. 8vo. R. Ingalton Drake, Eton. 1875.

Memoirs of Celebrated Etonians. By J. Heneage Jesse. 2 vols. Pp. 377, 354. 8vo. Bentley & Son, London. 1875.

Eton Thirty Years Since. By John Delaware Lewis ; and Letter on Above —in *Macmillan's Magazine,* May and July, 1875. Pp. 10. 8vo. Macmillan, London. 1875.

W. F. Taylor's Guide to Windsor, Eton and Virginia Water. Illustrated. Pp. 32. Obl. 12mo. W. F. Taylor. Windsor. 1875.

1875-6. The Etonian : 19th May, 1875, to 2nd August, 1876. [30 numbers.] Pp. 256. Sm. roy 8vo. R. Ingalton Drake, Eton. 1875-6.

1876. Eton College. Illustrated—in *Harper's New Monthly Magazine.* September, 1876. Pp. 10. Me. 8vo. Harper, New York. 1876.

Parodies Regained ; not by the Author of Parodies Lost. Pp. 16. Cr. 8vo. R. Ingalton Drake, Eton. 1876.

Eton College—in *Blackwood's Magazine*, March, 1876. Pp. 18. 8vo. Blackwood, Edinburgh. 1876.

The Recent Troubles at Eton College. By Robert P. Keep. Ph. D. Hartford, Conn.—in *The New Englander*, April, 1876. Pp. 9. 8vo. W. L. Kingsley, New Haven, Conn. 1876.

The Story of Valentine and his Brother. By Mrs. Oliphant. Pp. 440. Post 8vo. Blackwood, Edinburgh. 1876.

The Eton Portrait Gallery, consisting of Short Memoirs of the more Eminent Eton Men. By A Barrister of the Inner Temple. 12 engravings by Cavalier Gabriell. Pp. 581. 8vo. Williams & Son, Eton. 1876.

The Eton Tradition. By T. H. S. Escott—in *Belgravia*, Vol. XXIX., March, 1876. Pp. 10. 8vo. Chatto & Windus, London. 1876.

Eton. (From *All the Year Round*, N. S., vol. XVI., 20th May, 1876.) Pp. 7. 8vo. †

1877.   A History of Eton College: 1440-1875. By H. C. Maxwell-Lyte. Illustrated. New Issue, with Corrections. Pp. 535. Demy 8vo. Macmillan, London. 1877.

A Day of My Life, or Everyday Experiences at Eton. By An Eton Boy [G. Nugent Bankes]. Second Edition. Pp. 183. 12mo. Sampson Low & Co., London. 1877.

Out of School at Eton : being a Collection of Poetry and Prose Writings by some present Etonians. Pp. 150. 12mo. Sampson Low & Co. 1877.

Review of Lyte's "Eton College"—in *The Edinburgh Review*, October, 1877. Pp. 30. 8vo. A. & C. Black, Edinburgh. 1877.

Chords. By F. B. T. Money. Dedicated to Oscar Browning, late Assistant Master of Eton College. For Private Circulation. Pp. 316. Cr. 8vo. Civil Service Printing Co., London. 1877.

Eton College. By C. E. Pascoe. Illustrated—in *Appleton's Journal*, September, 1877. Pp. 6. Med. 8vo. D. Appleton, New York. 1877.

1878.   Eton College. Illustrated—in *The Leisure Hour*, June, 1878. Pp. 7. Royal 8vo. Religious Tract Society, London. 1878.

Memoir of the Rev. Francis Hodgson, B.D., Scholar, Poet and Divine. With numerous Letters from Lord Byron and others. 2 vols. Pp. 297, 347. Post 8vo. Macmillan, London. 1878.

John-A-Dreams : A Tale. By Julian Sturgis. Pp. 318. Sm. 8vo. Blackwood, Edinburgh. 1878.

1879. Praepostor's Book : Division XV. : May-June, 1879. Cr. 8vo.

A Sermon preached in Eton College Chapel by the Rev. Edmond Warre, in memory of Etonians fallen in the Zulu War. Pp. 15. Cr. 8vo. Williams, Eton College. 1879.

Our Public Schools, I. : Eton—in *The New Quarterly Magazine*, January, 1879. Pp. 23. Demy 8vo. C. Kegan Paul & Co., London. 1879.

Our Sons at Eton and Oxford. By A Parent. With Elucidations by One of the Sons—in *Fraser's Magazine*, December, 1879. Pp. 20. 8vo. Longmans, London. 1879.

1880. Athletics in Public Schools. By the Hon. and Rev. E. Lyttelton—in *The Nineteenth Century*, January, 1880. Pp. 15. 8vo. C. Kegan Paul & Co., London.

The Eton Boating Book. By R. H. Blake-Humphrey, 1875. An Appendix to the above. By R. H. Blake-Humphrey and G. C. Bourne. Pp. 298. Post 8vo. Williams & Son, Eton. 1880.

The Eton Rambler. 6 numbers [all published]. Pp. 44. Royal 8vo. R. Ingalton Drake, Eton. 1880.

1881. Eton College Library. Reprinted from *Notes and Queries*. By the Rev. Francis St. John Thackeray. Pp. 100. Sq. 8vo. Williams & Son, Eton. 1881.

Rambles about Eton. By Alfred Rimmer. Illustrated—in *Belgravia*, January, February, March, June, 1881. Pp. 51. 8vo. Chatto & Windus, London. 1881.

A Tale of Granada—the Seasons. By A Present Etonian. 1881.†

Everyday Life in our Public Schools. Edited by Charles Eyre Pascoe. Pp. 314. Cr. 8vo. Griffith & Farran, London. 1881.

Our Public Schools. Pp. 373. Post 8vo. Kegan Paul & Co., London. 1881.

1882.   Rambles Round Eton and Harrow. By Alfred Rimmer. With 52 Illustrations. [Also An *Edition de Luxe.*] Pp. 290. Chatto & Windus, London. 1882.

An Eton Boy. By Matthew Arnold—in *The Fortnightly Review*, June, 1882. Pp. 15. Med. 8vo. Chapman & Hall, London. 1882.

Dick's Wandering. By Julian Sturgis. 3 vols. Pp. 256, 251, 244. Post 8vo. Blackwood, London. 1882.

The Thames: Oxford to London : Twenty Etched Plates by David Law. Pp. 40. Folio. G. Bell, London. 1882.

A Guide to the Collection of Roman Coins at Eton College, with an Appendix on Some Byzantine Coins. By the late F. St. J. Thackeray. Pp. 92. Sm. post 8vo. R. Ingalton Drake, Eton. 1882.

Life At Home, At School, At College. By A Present Etonian. Plates. Cr. 8vo. Swan Sonnenschein & Co., London. 1882.

1882-3.   The Eton College Rifle Volunteer Gazette. No. 1. (6th December, 1882), No. 2 (6th December, 1883). Pp. 20. Royal 4to. R. Ingalton Drake, Eton. 1882-3.

1883.   Eton Manuscripts: Ninth Report, Historical MSS. Commission. Part I. Pp. 10. Sm. Folio [Blue Book]. Eyre & Spottiswoode, London. 1883.

How I Stole the Block. By An Old Etonian. Pp. 16. Cr. 8vo. Bickers, London. 1883.

Seven Years at Eton : 1857-1864. By James Brinsley-Richards. Pp. 447. Sm. post 8vo. [4 editions in 1883]. Bentley & Son, London. 1883.

Records of An Eton School Boy. Edited by Charles Milnes Gaskell. With a Preface by Sir Francis Doyle, Bart. Pp. 180. Post 8vo. Privately printed.] 1883.

Mr. Gladstone's Schooldays. By J. Brinsley-Richards. (From *Temple Bar*, February, 1883.) Pp. 20. 8vo. R. Bentley, London. 1883.

1883-5.   The Etonian. 29 Numbers (all published). Sm. royal 8vo. Ingalton Drake, Eton. 1883-85.

1884. "Collegers v. Oppidans": A Reminiscence of Eton Life. By An Old
Etonian. Pp. 84. Sq. 16mo. R. Ingalton Drake, Eton. 1884.

Eton: As She is not. By J. Goodwin. Illustrated by Sir D. Carlyon-
Max. Pp. 51. Sq. 16mo. R. Ingalton Drake, Eton. 1384.

The Eton Days of Sir Stafford Northcote. (From *Temple Bar*, January,
1884.) Pp. 14. 8vo. R. Bentley, London. 1884.

A Visit to Eton. By Mowbray Morris — in *The English Illustrated
Magazine*, November, 1884. Pp. 15. Royal 8vo. Macmillan & Co.,
London. 1884.

Some Early Writings of Shelley. By Prof. Edward Dowden—in *The
Contemporary Review*, September, 1884. Pp. 14. Med. 8vo. Isbister,
London.

1885. The Royal River : The Thames from Source to Sea, descriptive, historical,
pictorial. Illustrated. Pp. 368. Roy. 4to. Cassell & Co., London.
1885.

The Eton School Lists: from 1791 to 1877, with Notes and Index by
H. E. C. Stapylton. Pp. 415. Sq. cr. 8vo. R. Ingalton Drake, Eton.
1885.

Sketchy Memories of Eton : 1866-1872. By "Mac". Pp. 48. 12mo.
Thacker, Sqink & Co., Calcutta. 1885.

Some Views and Opinions of Sparrow on Housetops. Extracted by
"Peccator Maximus". Illustrated. Pp. 42. Impl. 8vo. R. Ingalton
Drake, Eton. 1885.

Noblesse Oblige: A Plea for the Preservation of Eton Buildings ; with
Other Matters. Pp. 19. Roy. 8vo. Privately printed. R. Ingalton
Drake, Eton. 1885.

Confessions of an Eton Master. By H. S. Salt. (From *The Nineteenth
Century*, January, 1885.) Pp. 15. Med. 8vo. C. Kegan Paul & Co.,
London. 1885.

The Eton Tutorial System. By the Earl of Darnley—in *The Nineteenth
Century*, March, 1885. Pp. 10. Med. 8vo. C. Kegan Paul & Co.,
London. 1885.

Eton in Eighty-five. By G. E. Marindin—in *The Fortnightly Review*,
June, 1885. Pp. 13. Med. 8vo. Chapman & Hall, London. 1885.

Eton Reform. By F. W. Cornish—in *The Nineteenth Century*, October, 1885. Pp. 16. Med. 8vo. C. Kegan Paul & Co., London. 1885.

A Certain Eton Boy [Thomas Arne]. By E. C. Needham. (From *London Society*, March, 1885.) Pp. 8. 8vo. 51 Great Queen Street, London. 1885.

1886. The Architectural History of the University of Cambridge and of the Colleges of Cambridge and Eton. By the late Robert Willis. Edited, with large additions, by John Willis Clark, M.A. Illustrated. Vol. I. Part II. (vii.) [Eton]. Pp. 452. Roy. 8vo. University Press, Cambridge. 1886.

Windsor: A Description of the Castle, Park, Town and Neighbourhood. By W. J. Loftie. Illustrated. Pp. 91. Imp. 4to. Seely & Co., London. 1886.

Education and Eton College—in *The Church Quarterly Review*, January, 1886. Pp. 10. 8vo. Spottiswoode & Co., London. 1886.

Extracts from the Speeches of George Canning, with Illustrative Comments on some Parts of his Life. A Lecture delivered in the School Library at Eton, 22nd May. Pp. 34. "The Least shall be Great": a Sermon preached in the Chapel of Eton College, 23rd May, by Henry Montagu Butler, D.D., Dean of Gloucester and late Head Master of Harrow School. Pp. 10. Cr. 8vo. R. Ingalton Drake, Eton. 1886.

Eton Worthies. By Walter Herries Pollock—in *The Fortnightly Review*, June, 1886. Pp. 6. Med. 8vo. Chapman & Hall, London. 1886.

Old Eton Days—in *All the Year Round*, N. S., Vol. XXXIX., November, 1886. Roy. 8vo. Bradbury & Agnew, London. 1886.

The Eton Review: Conducted by Present Etonians. 10 numbers. Pp. 84. Sq. roy. 8vo. R. Ingalton Drake, Eton. 1886.

Eton Masters Forty Years Ago. By W. C. Green—in *The Churchman*, December, 1886. Pp. 10. 8vo. Elliot Stock, London. 1886.

1887. The Eton Fortnightly: Conducted by Present Etonians. 10 numbers [all published]. Pp. 80. Royal 8vo. R. Ingalton Drake, Eton. 1887.

Vert de Vert's Eton Days and Other Memories. By the Rev. A. G. L'Estrange. Pp. 294. Cr. 8vo. Elliot Stock, London. 1887.

The Eton Observer. 2 numbers [all published]. Pp. 16. Roy. 8vo. R. Ingalton Drake, Eton. March, 1887.

How I Spent my Summer Holidays in 1876. By An Eton Boy. Pp. 36. Sm. 12mo. R. Ingalton Drake, Eton. 1887.

1888. Some Distant Prospects of Eton College—in *Macmillan's Magazine*, Jan., 1888. Pp. 9. 8vo. Macmillan, London. 1888.

Eton : 1836 to 1841. By C. T. Buckland—in *Longmans' Magazine*, June, 1888. Pp. 11. 8vo. Longmans, London. 1888.

A Midsummer Night Dream. By E. V. B. Illustrated. Pp. 30. Sm. roy. 8vo. R. Ingalton Drake, Eton. 1888.

Percy Bysshe Shelley : A Monograph. By H. S. Salt late Assistant Master at Eton]. Portrait. Pp. 277. Folio 8vo. Swan Sonnenschein & Co., London. 1888.

A Memoir of Henry Bradshaw, Fellow of King's College, Cambridge, and University Librarian. Illustrated. Pp. 447. Demy 8vo. Kegan Paul, Trench & Co., London. 1888.

Reminiscences of Eton (Keate's Time). By the Rev. C. Allix Wilkinson. Illustrated. Pp. 340. Post 8vo. Hurst & Blackett, London. 1888.

Dorica. By E. D. Stone. Pp. 173. Sm. post 8vo. C. Kegan Paul, Trench & Co., London. 1888.

The Present Etonian. 15 numbers [all published]. Pp. 120. Sq. roy. 8vo. R. Ingalton Drake, Eton. 1888.

Reminiscences of William Rogers, Rector of St. Botolph, Bishopsgate. Compiled by R. H. Hadden. Illustrated. Pp. 228. Post 8vo. Kegan Paul & Co. 1888.

A Year Ago. By Lennox Barnhill. Pp. 23. Post 8vo. R. Ingalton Drake, Eton. 22nd June, 1888.

Note Book of the Shelley Society. Edited by the Honorary Secretaries. Part I. Vol. I. Pp. 213. Demy 8vo. Reeves & Turner, London. 1888.

1889. The Eton Review : Conducted by Present Etonians. 10 numbers [all pub.]. Pp. 80. Sq. roy. 8vo. R. Ingalton Drake, Eton. 1889.

The History of Eton College : 1440-1884. By H. C. Maxwell-Lyte. Illustrated. A New Edition, Revised and Enlarged. Pp. 543 Demy 8vo. Macmillan & Co., London. 1889.

Cyril: a romantic novel. By Geoffrey Drayc. Pp. 796. Cr. 8vo. W. H. Allan & Co., London. 1889. Reprinted.

The Parachute: Directed by Present Etonians. 3 numbers (complete). No. 1, 22nd June; No. 2, 6th July; No. 3, 30th July. Pp. 28. Roy. 8vo. R. Ingalton Drake, Eton. 1889.

Eton Fifty Years Ago. By C. T. Buckland—in *Macmillan's Magazine*, November, 1889. Pp. 9. 8vo. Macmillan & Co., London. 1889.

Bishop Selwyn, of New Zealand and Lichfield: a sketch of his life and work. By G. H. Curteis. Pp. 498. Cr. 8vo. Kegan Paul & Co., London. 1889.

1890. Seven Summers: An Eton Medley. By the Editors of *The Parachute* and *Present Etonian*. Pp. 192, Sm. post 8vo. R. Ingalton Drake, Eton. 1890.

Eton College: a Review of Maxwell-Lyte's " History of Eton College "—in *The Quarterly Review*, July, 1890. Pp. 27. 8vo. Murray, London. 1890.

Eton College. 1. Historical and Descriptive, by H. C. Maxwell-Lyte; 2. Athletics, by the Rev. Sydney R. James; 3. As a School, by the Hon. Alfred Lyttelton. Illustrated—in *The English Illustrated Magazine*, July, 1890. Pp. 19. Roy. 8vo. Macmillan, London. 1890.

About some Fellows: or Odds and Ends from my Note Book. By An Eton Boy [G. Nugent Bankes]. *New Edition*. Pp. 203. Sq. 16mo. S. Low & Co., London. 1890.

The Rocket: Conducted by Present Etonians. Pp. 12. Cr. 8vo. R. Ingalton Drake, Eton. 31st March, 1890.

Rowing at Westminster from 1813 to 1883: Extracted from the School Water Ledgers. Illustrated. Pp. 137. Post 8vo. Kegan Paul & Co., London. 1890.

Song of the Football Cup. Written by R. Carr Bosanquet; the Music composed by Joseph Barnby. Pp. 11. Roy. 12mo. R. Ingalton Drake, Eton. 1890.

1891. A Sermon preached by Richard, Lord Bishop of Chichester [Durnford], at the Consecration of the Lower Chapel, Eton College. Pp. 10. Sm. 8vo. Eton College Press, 24th June, 1891.

Keat's Lane Papers: an Eton Miscellany. Pp. 36. Obl. 12mo. George New, Eton. 1891.

Henry VI. : A Lecture delivered at Eton by C. R. L. Fletcher. Pp. 38. Cr. 8vo. R. Ingalton Drake, Eton. 5th December, 1891.

The Stream of Pleasure: a Narrative of a Journey on the Thames from Oxford to London. By Joseph and Elizabeth Pennell. Together with a practical chapter by J. J. Legge. Pp. 160. Sq. cr. 8vo. T. Fisher Unwin, London. 1891.

The Thames: from Oxford to the Tower. By William Senior (Red Spinner). Illustrated by Francis S. Walker. Pp. 120. Demy 4to. J. C. Nimmo, London. 1891.

Boating. By W. B. Woodgate ; with a Chapter on Rowing at Eton by R. Harvey Mason. Illustrated. [Badminton Library.] Pp. 352. Cr. 8vo. Longmans, London. 1891.

Eton Montem: a Memory of the Past. By G. C. Green—in *Blackwood's Magazine*, September, 1891. Pp. 10. 8vo. Blackwood, Edinburgh. 1891.

The Student's Humour : conducted by XX Present Etonians. Pp. 8. Roy. 8vo. R. Ingalton Drake, Eton. 4th June, 1891.

The Mayfly : directed by Present Etonians. 3 numbers [all published]. No. 1, 16th May ; No. 2, 4th June; No. 3, 24th June. Pp. 24. Roy. 8vo. R. Ingalton Drake, Eton. 1891.

Eton Loan Collection Catalogues. Edited by F. H. Rawlins. Pp. 96. Sm. 8vo. R. Ingalton Drake, Eton. 1891. Second Edition. Pp. 108. Roy 8vo. *idem*. 1891.

Catalogue of Loan Collection of Portraits, Views and other Objects of Interest connected with the History of Eton, made on the occasion of the 450th Anniversary of the Foundation of the College. By F. H. Rawlins. Third Edition, Revised and Enlarged. Large Paper (250 copies). Pp. 122. Demy 4to. R. Ingalton Drake, Eton. 1891.

Flosculi Etonenses: 1880-1891. Pp. 35. 12mo. Eton College Press. *n.d.*

Camp Choruses. E. C. R. Volunteers. Compiled by Walter Durnford. The Hon. John Baring. With Appendix. Pp. 86. Sm. 32mo. R. Ingalton Drake, Eton. 1891.

Founders' Day : a Secular Ode on the Ninth Jubilee of Eton College. By
R. Bridges. Pp. 7. Sq. 8vo. [Privately printed.] 1891.

Lapsus Calami. By J. K. Stephen. Pp. 88. 12mo. Macmillan &
Bowes, Cambridge. 1891. Second Edition, 1891. New Edition [the
Third]. [Also Large Paper.] Pp. 92. 1891.

Eton College Jubilee: I. Consecration of Lower Chapel ; II. Programme ;
III. Thanksgiving Service ; IV. A. M. Goodhart's "Arethusa" ; V.
C. H. H. Parry's " Eton ". Roy 8vo. 1891.

The Eton Jubilee. By A. C. Benson—in *The National Review*, July, 1891.
Pp. 15. Med. 8vo. W. H. Allan & Co., London. 1891.

Quo Musa Tendis? By J. K. Stephen. Pp. 84. 12mo. Macmillan &
Bowes, Cambridge. 1891.

Tim. [A tale of school life.] Pp. 318. Cr. 8vo. Macmillan & Co.,
London. 1891.

Leaves from a Note-book on Some School Days — in *Macmillan's
Magazine*, February, 1891. Pp. 8. 1891.

Ionica. By W. Cory. *New Edition.* Pp. 210. 12mo. George Allen,
London. 1891.

A Few Hints on Cricket. Pp. 16. 1887. Eton Cricket. By R. A. H.
Mitchell. Pp. 22. Sm. 8vo. R. Ingalton Drake. January, 1892.

1891-2. Eton Songs. By A. C. Ainger and J. Barnby. Illustrated by Herbert
Marshall. Pp. 148. Roy. 4to. Leadenhall Press, London. 1891-2.

1892. Dunwell Parva. By Reginald Lucas. Pp. 190. Post 8vo. Warne &
Co., London. 1892.

Le Cahier Jaune: Poems. By Arthur Christopher Benson, of Eton
College. Pp. 99. 8vo. [Privately printed.] George New, Eton. 1892.

Eton of Old, or Eighty Years Ago : 1811-1822. By An Old Colleger.
Eton of To-day. By A Modern. Illustrated. [Large Paper Edition,
250 copies.] Pp. 244. Roy. 8vo. Griffith & Farran, London. 1892.

Væ Victis: or 'Tis Sixty Years Since : an Eton Reminiscence. By A
Grandfather. Illustrated. Pp. 19. Sm. post 8vo. R. Ingalton Drake,
Eton. 1892.

Rules of the Wall Game as played at Eton. 1885. Rules of the Game of
Fives as played at Eton. 1889. Rules of the Game of Football as

played in "The Field" at Eton. Pp. 47. 32mo. R. Ingalton Drake. Eton. 1892.

The Grosvenor Guide to the Latin Prose Paper, or Latin as she is wrote, for the advantage of Pandufferdom, at which we dedicate him particularly. By Philoduff. Under the kind patronage of the Lower Master. Second Edition, with improvements and illustrations. Pp. 31. Sq. 8vo. R. Ingalton Drake, Eton. 1892.

Eton. By Oscar Browning—in *Picturesque Europe*. Part II. Pp. 13. Royal 4to. 1892.

The Training of Boys at Eton. By A. C. Benson—in *The Forum*, June, 1892. Pp. 11. Roy. 8vo. 1892.

Stories of Old Etonian Days. By C. Kegan Paul—in *The Nineteenth Century*, October, 1892. Pp. 10. 1892.

Young England at School : Eton College. By W. C. Sargent—in the *Ludgate Monthly*, November, 1892. Pp. 10. Med. 8vo. 1892.

Eton and the Empire: an Address delivered at Eton College. By Geoffrey Drage. Saturday, 13th November, 1890. Pp. 40. Post 8vo. R. Ingalton Drake, Eton. 1892.

Sir Henry Wotton : Gentleman and Schoolmaster—in *Littel's Living Age*, May, 1892. By Foster Watson. Pp. 10. Demy 8vo. Littell, Boston, U.S.A.

1893. Eton School Songs: Words by Arthur Benson : Music by Arthur Goodhart. 1. Song of the Scug [J. K. Stephen] ; 2. The Eton College Hunt ; 3. The Game's the Thing ; 4. Song of the Wall ; 5. No Triumphs like those ; 6. Twenty Years Ago. Pp. 44. Roy. 8vo. Novello, Ewer & Co., London. 1893.

Poems. By Arthur Christopher Benson. Pp. 192. 12mo. Mathews & Lane, London. 1893.

Some Eton Translations: 1827. By W. E. Gladstone (*ætat.* 18)—in *The Contemporary Review*, June, 1893. Pp. 8. Med. 8vo. Isbister, London. 1893.

The Eton Idler : a Miscellany. 22nd May, to 1st August, 1893. 7 numbers (all published). Pp. 56. 4to. R. Ingalton Drake, Eton. 1893.

A Memoir of the Rev. James Lonsdale, late Fellow and Tutor of Balliol

College, Oxford.   By Russell Duckworth, B.A., Trinity College, Cam-
bridge.   With an Introduction by the Hon. G. C. Brodrick, Warden of
Merton College, Oxford.   Illustrated.   Pp. 264.   Cr. 8vo.   Longmans
& Co., London.   1893.

The Eton Spectator.   3 numbers (all published).   Pp. 12.   Sq. 8vo.   R.
Ingalton Drake, Eton.   1893.

Idyll: Walking by the Mail.   22nd December, 1893.   Pp. 8.   Post 8vo.
Privately printed.

1894.   Eton School Songs: Words by A. C. Ainger; Music by J. Barnby.   1.
Carmen Etonense; 2. *Vale;* 3. The River Song; 4. Cricket Song; 5.
Football Song; 6. Fives Song [music by C. H. Lloyd]; 7. Volunteer
Song.   Pp. 57.   Roy. 8vo.   Novello, Ewer & Co.. London.   1894.

The New Floreat: a Letter to an Eton Boy on the Social Question.   By
the Rev. James Adderley, author of Stephen Remarx.   Pp. 96.   12mo.
Wells, Gardner & Darton, London.   1894.

Eton and the Labour Question.   By Geoffrey Drage.   Pp. 37.   Sm. 8vo.
26th May, 1894.

Eton Cricket.   By the Hon. R. H. Lyttelton—in *The National Review,*
May, 1894.   Pp. 9.   Med. 8vo.   W. H. Allen & Co., London.   1894.

Etoniana.   By Walter Durnford—in *The National Review,* November,
1894.   Pp. 8.   Med. 8vo.   Edward Arnold, London.   1894.

Great Public Schools: Eton, Harrow, Charterhouse, Cheltenham, Rugby,
Clifton, Westminster, Marlborough, Haileybury, Winchester.   Illustrated.   Pp. 344.   Cr. 8vo.   Edward Arnold, London.   1894.

An Eton Master—in *Blackwood's Magazine.*   November, 1894.   Pp. 7.
8vo.   Blackwood, Edinburgh.   1894.

1850-94.   Notes concerning Eton College: copied from *Notes and Queries.*   1850-
94.   [MS.]   Pp. 70.   Sq. 8vo.

1895.   Etonians at Ascot.   Illustrated—in Finch Mason's *Sporting Annual,*
January, 1895.   Pp. 4.   Imp. 8vo.   Simpkin & Co., London.   1895.

Deucalionea: or Autumn Episodes of Eton, 1894.   By Arthur C. James.
With Illustrations by the Old Masters.   Pp. 24.   Royal 8vo.   George
New, Eton.   1895.

Thomas Gray. By Arthur Christopher Benson, of Eton College. Pp. 10. Sq. roy. 8vo. [Privately printed.] R. Ingalton Drake, Eton. 1895.

Lyrics. By Arthur Christopher Benson. Pp. 189. 12mo. John Lane, London. 1895.

A Descriptive Catalogue of the MSS. in the Library of Eton College. By Montague Rhodes James, Litt. D., Fellow of King's College, Cambridge, Director of the Fitzwilliam Museum. Pp. 125. Roy. 8vo. University Press, Cambridge. 1895.

Preces in Schola Collegii Regalis Apud Etonam Recitæ. Londini, 1686. Reprinted. Chiswick Press, London. 1895. Pp. 23. 12mo.

The Professor. By Arthur Christopher Benson, of Eton College. Pp. 51. Imp. 8vo. G. New, Eton. 1895.

Babylonica. By Arthur Christopher Benson, of Eton College. Illustrated. Pp. 20. Sq. post 8vo. G. New, Eton. 1895.

The New Etonian. 4 numbers (all published). Illustrated. Pp. 32. Roy 8vo. R. Ingalton Drake, Eton. 1895.

The Old Etonian Football Club. Pp. 88. Sq. 32mo. Blades, East & Blades, London. 1895.

Reminiscences. By John Joel. Pp. 22. 12mo. R. Ingalton Drake, Eton. 1895.

Walks round about Eton and Eton Buildings. By James J. Hornby. Illustrated. Pp. 80. Demy 8vo. R. Ingalton Drake, Eton. 1895.

Great Names at Eton and Harrow—in *The Strand Magazine*, November 1895. Pp. 6. 8vo. G. Newnes, London. 1895.

1896. Poems and Translations. Pp. 44. 12mo. Blackwell, Oxford. 1896.

Upper Club. By Reginald Lucas—in *The Badminton Magazine*, May, 1896. Pp. 12. 8vo. Longmans, London. 1896.

An Eton Playing Field: a Reminiscence of Happy Days spent at the Eton Mission. By E. M. S. Pilkington. With a memorandum by C. J. Kekewich. Pp. 128. Obl. 12mo. E. Arnold, London. 1896.

Memoir of Edward Craven Hawtrey, D.D., Head Master and afterwards Provost of Eton. By Francis St. John Thackeray. Illustrated. Pp. 267. Sm. post 8vo. G. Bell & Sons, London. 1896.

Eton in the Forties. By an Old Colleger [Arthur Duke Coleridge]. Illustrated. Pp. 395. Post 8vo. R. Bentley, London. 1896.

Games at Eton.   By F. B. Elliott.   Illustrated—in *The Badminton Magazine*, December, 1896.   Pp. 14.   Demy 8vo.   Longmans & Co., London.   1896.

The Plautus of Aristophanes up to date : or, " Mammon made righteous ". By Arthur C. James, M.A.   Pp. 50.   Sq. roy. 8vo.   R. Ingalton Drake, Eton.   1896.

1897.   The Chiltern Hundreds.   By Albert J. Foster.   Illustrated.   Pp. 220. Post 8vo.   J. S. Virtue, London.   1897.

Fourth of June Celebration : Souvenir of the Diamond Jubilee Year. Views and Programme.   Pp. 8.   Obl. 12mo.   *Chronicle* Office, Windsor.   1897.

Sermons preached in Eton College Chapel, 1870-1897.   By Francis St John Thackeray.   Cr. 8vo.   George Bell and Sons, London.   1897.

Old Eton and Modern Public Schools—In *The Edinburgh Review*, April, 1897.   Pp. 27.   8vo.   Longman, 1897.

Extracts from the Letters and Journals of William Cory, author of " Ionica ".   Selected and arranged by Francis Warre Cornish.   Pp. 586. Cr. 8vo.   *Priv. prin.*   1897.

UNDATED AND DATES NOT KNOWN.

Eton.   (From Charles Knight's *Pictorial Half-Hours*, Vol. IV.)   Illustrated.   Pp. 5.   Sq. post 8vo.   C. Knight, London.

The Visitors' Handbook to Windsor, Eton and Virginia Water.   Pp. 64.   12mo. Cradock & Co., London.   *n.d.*

Eighty Picturesque Views of the Thames and Medway : Historical Descriptions by W. G. Fearnside.   Pp. 84.   Impl. 8vo.   Black & Armstrong, London.   *n.d.*

The Land we live in : a Pictorial and Literary Sketch-book of the British Empire.   By Charles Knight.   Vol. II. :   Windsor and Eton.   Pp. 74. Imp. 8vo.

Poems : By A Young Gentleman at Eton School (under sixteen years of age). Pp. 15.   Cr. 8vo.   Mr. Lander, Eton.   *n.d.*

The Thames from its Rise to the Nore. By Walter Armstrong, M.A. Illustrated. Pp. 176. 4to. Virtue & Co., Ltd., London. *n.d.*

An Elegy, written in memory of a Young Lady who died by accident two days before her intended marriage. By An Etonian. Pp. 8. Roy. 8vo. C. Knight, Windsor.

A Review of the Changes made at Eton since February, 1864. Pp. 19. Cr. 8vo. *n.d.*

Manuscripts.

(Copied from papers in the possession of Sir J. Buchanan Riddell, Bart.)

NUGÆ ETONENSES. Pp. 17. Sq. roy. 8vo.

1. *Nugæ Etonenses. c.* 1765-6 ;
2. Bill at Maidenhead of the Boys' Rebellion, 2nd November, 1768 ;
3. Business of 4th Form and Remove, *c.* 1824 ;
4. Expenses of a Colleger at Eton, 1824-49 ;
5. Alcaics [supposed to be by the Marquess of Wellesley ;
6. Greek verses, by Luxmoore.